the
HORSE
in
art

the
HORSE
in
art

By Ruth Zuelke, Designed by Robert Clark Nelson ■ Lerner Publications Company, Minneapolis, Minn.

Horse and Bridle, by Peter Paul Rubens; Albertina, Vienna.

Introduction

As long as man has existed, he has known the horse. Prehistoric people who had no written language have told us about horses through their art. *Archaeologists* (AHR-kee-AHL-uh-jists), who study old ruins, skeletons and man-made objects or *artifacts*, can usually tell a great deal about the people who lived thousands of years ago. They have many ways of discovering facts, but one of the best ways is through the art works they find.

Art is truly a universal language. By looking today at a picture or a carving made many years ago we can get a feeling of how people lived and what was important to them. The horse first appeared in art about 30,000 years ago. Horses are shown in art all through the ages. This alone tells us how important a part of man's life the horse has been.

The way in which the horse is portrayed tells us how the artist felt about it. As you go through this book, let the artists speak to you.

Horse Sculpture, Archaic; Uffizi Gallery, Florence; Photo Alinari.

A group of clay tablets were found recently by archaeologists in Turkey. The tablets seemed to have been part of a book of rules or a textbook on horseback riding. This tablet shows us a man on horseback that was made by a Hittite artist. The Hittites were a powerful people who lived more than 4,000 years ago in the area of modern Turkey.

This picture of horses is 30,000 years old. It was found in the Lascaux (lass-coh) caves in Southern France. These are the earliest works of art still existing today which show horses. The pictures in the caves were painted on the walls with black, red, yellow and brown earth. We think that the colored earth may have been mixed with birds' eggs to help it stick to the walls.

Do you notice that the bodies of the horses are larger and the legs are shorter than those of our horses today? Bones have been found which show that the horses were shaped differently from ours. We can hardly say that they are graceful, but we might call them noble and fierce. Archaeologists believe that these horses were hunted for food.

Painting from Lascaux Cave, 28,000 BC; Lascaux, France.

Hittite Tablet, About 2000 BC; State Museum, Berlin.

This little statuette of horse and rider was found in an ancient Egyptian tomb and is about 3,500 years old. The statuette is about 12 inches long. It is carved of wood, and the lines are made with white paint. It is thought to represent a groom who took care of the horses.

Ancient Egyptians believed in a life after death. The mummies we see in museums today are the preserved bodies of important people of ancient Egypt. The people of that time were sure that the souls of the dead would need their preserved bodies in the other world. Egyptians placed in the tombs all the things a rich man and his family might need in after-life, including food, household utensils, clothing and jewels. They also buried models of servants and animals.

Some of the most famous tombs are in the great pyramids that are still standing today. Pyramids were built for kings and their families. Entrances to the tombs were hidden, but grave-robbers often found their way in to steal treasures during the thousands of years since the tombs were built. Archaeologists have found several tombs that had not been robbed, and the contents of these are now in museums. Archaeologists believe that the Egyptians were able to develop their art and science so highly because the rich soil and warm climate along the banks of the Nile made it easy to grow food. This left more time for other activities. The Egyptian Bronze age began more than 5,000 years ago.

Horse and Groom, about 1500 BC; Metropolitan Museum of Art, New York, Rogers Fund.

This horse and chariot was made of bronze with gold decorations. It was used more than 3,000 years ago by the Danes in their sun-worship ceremonies.

The Bronze Age is the name of the prehistoric period when people discovered that bronze made better tools and weapons than the stone that they had been using until then. The Bronze Age came at different times in different parts of the world. Archaeologists think that prehistoric peoples may have discovered metals when the campfires, which they built again and again in the same spot, finally melted the metal out of the rock of their fireplaces.

Bronze is a very hard, durable metal made of a mixture of tin and copper. Artists still use it today for their sculpture.

Horse and Chariot, 1300-1000 BC, Danish National Museum, Copenhagen.

Painting, Tomb of Menna, 1420-1411 BC; Oriental Institute, University of Chicago.

This wall painting is from an Egyptian tomb. The human figure is drawn in the style that Egyptian artists used for thousands of years. It shows the side view of the head, the front view of the trunk or torso and the side view of the arms and legs. Animals were usually drawn more as they appeared in real life, although several horses shown together often looked as if they were drawn one on top of the other. If you look back at the statuette of the groom on horseback, you can see that early Egyptian sculpture in the round is more graceful than the drawings made by artists during the same period.

Archaeologists tell us that Egyptian horses pulled chariots in battles and in religious and triumphal processions. Horses were not used in farming or ridden for sport until later. The horses and chariot seen here may have been used to carry an important person to a harvest.

Clay has been used by many artists through the centuries. Archaeologists date these three horses from about 2,500 or 3,000 years ago. They say that they *date* an object when they estimate how old it is.

The horses were found in Cyprus, an island in the Mediterranean. They are made of *terracotta*, a baked clay. The Cypriot horses look as if the clay had been rolled and pinched into shape. The way an artifact is made and how the finished object looks is called its *style*.

Cypriot Horses, about 1000-600 BC; Metropolitan Museum of Art, New York, Cesnola Collection.

The Assyrians learned about *equestrianism* (e-KWES-tree-un-ism), or the art of riding, from the Hittites. The land in which the Assyrians lived has had many names. One of the more well-known names is Mesopotamia. It lay between the Tigris and Euphrates rivers, in the area of present-day Iraq, Syria and Turkey. Babylon and Ninevah were two of its cities famous during Biblical times. Artists in Mesopotamia used clay and stone in their work. We see the brave deeds of their kings in hunting and in war illustrated in *extant* art, or works of art that still exist.

One such brave king was Assurbanipal (AH-shoor-BAH-ne-pahl). He ruled in Ninevah from 668 to 630 BC, more than 2,500 years ago. King Assurbanipal is shown hunting lions. The other sculpture portrays part of his ceremonial procession.

These relief sculptures were made by carving the stone away from the background so that the figures stand out. The Assyrian artists expressed more power in their horses than the Egyptians did in theirs. Note the emphasis placed on the bones and muscles. The bridle and harness are decorative, and the manes of the horses are braided and waved.

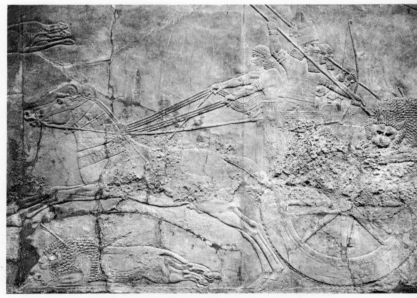

King Assurbanipal Hunting Lions, about 668 BC; British Museum, London.

Assyrian Procession, about 600 BC; Louvre, Paris, Photo Alinari.

Horses and riders were still shown frequently in Assyrian art of the early 7th century AD, approximately 1,200 years later than the relief sculpture of King Assurbanipal. This woven piece of silk showing two men on horseback came from Syria. It was woven on a loom not too different from those used by hand-weavers today.

Persia was another country in the area of the Tigris and Euphrates, to which we now refer as the Near or Middle East. Perox I, a king who lived from 459 to 484 AD, is shown here shooting *ibexes,* a form of wild goat, with bow and arrow.

This silver emblem is about eight and one-half inches in diameter. It illustrates the skill many silversmiths possessed approximately 1,500 years ago. It's easy to imagine the speed of the arrow shot by King Perox.

Syrian Textile, about 700 AD;
Metropolitan Museum of Art, New York, Fletcher Fund.

Persian Silver Disk of Perox I, 226-637 AD;
Metropolitan Museum of Art, New York, Fletcher Fund.

بهشیادی وفدرکیشت | یا کسان من یک یک اوجکت | مکرد از فروما یکی کردجهان | که نشند کا سکردزنرکان | افزاده ومردم رای زن | کشی بشت رنی نامدار انجمن

Battle of Ardashir and Arduan, 14th Century AD; Detroit Institute of Arts.

When the Moslems conquered Persia in 641 AD, all animal design was prohibited by the Moslem religion. For this reason Persian art showed no horses for many years. The ruling was gradually relaxed, and people and animals began to appear in the *miniatures* or small drawings which were made on manuscripts. The miniatures were made with pens and black ink. They were painted with watercolor and accented with touches of gold. Our interest is in looking at the picture on this page. But at the time the artist created this book, the beautiful Arabic handwriting or *calligraphy* (cuh-LIG-ruh-fee) was considered the more important of the two arts.

If you examine this Persian miniature closely you can see four horses. The artist who created this arrangement used circular lines that all had a common center of interest. This is called a *concentric* design. In fact, when you really inspect these four horses you cannot find anything but curved lines. Sometimes artists set problems for themselves and then attempt to solve them. This artist has been most successful in solving a problem in concentric design.

Four Horses, Early 17th Century; Courtesy, Museum of Fine Arts, Boston.

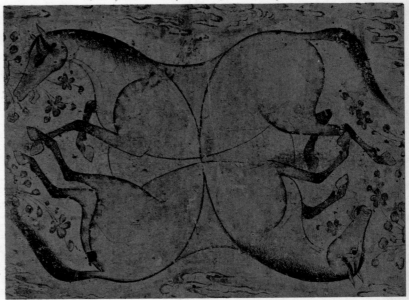

This is a painting of Shah Jahan (juh-HAHN), who had the famous Taj Mahal built. It is a miniature painted in an album designed by an artist that Shah Jahan may have brought to India from Persia.

The highly decorative horse wears as many jewels as the Shah himself. If you look at the middle of the background you can see a multitude of horsemen cantering in the same direction as the Shah. The angels in the sky are smiling happily on the Shah and his horse. The idea of angels may have been imported. India borrowed ideas from many parts of the world.

Portrait of Shah Jahan on Horseback, 1628-1658;
Metropolitan Museum of Art, New York, Gift of Alexander Smith Cochran.

Marruzou

n on Horseback, Parthenon 447-432 BC; British Museum, London.

A very different style of art, called *classical,* developed in Greece 2,000 years ago. Classical art expressed the Greek idea of perfection in whatever the subject might be—a horse, a human or a building.

Today we can still see one of the most beautiful buildings ever designed by any architect. Phidias (FID-ee-us) designed and supervised the construction of the *Parthenon,* a temple built for worship of the Greek goddess Athena. This building was erected during a period of great interest in the arts when Pericles (PEAR-i-klees) was the ruler in Athens, an important Greek city. The Parthenon was built of marble and still stands on a hill overlooking modern Athens. The Parthenon is one of a group of buildings called the Acropolis.

We can still see what a beautiful construction the Parthenon must have been at the time it was built in 447 BC. Phidias had an overall plan that took 11 years to complete. Many artists worked with him carving the marble sculpture with which the building was decorated.

The Parthenon, 447-432 BC.

This head is part of a large sculptural group that was on the east end of the Parthenon. It contained four horses and a chariot. The chariot was for Selene, the Greek goddess of the moon. Much of the work has been lost, but this head shows us how graceful the entire group must have been. Phidias planned that anyone looking at it would get the impression that the four marble horses were sinking below the horizon when the moon began to set. It's not hard to imagine the feeling of speed that four such horses would give the viewers.

Young Men on Horseback is part of the relief sculpture that circled around the outer walls of the Parthenon, under the roof. A continuing band of decoration is called a *frieze* (frees). This portion is on the north side of the building. It tells a story about a procession of men and women who marched from the foot of the Acropolis up to the Parthenon. This segment is near the end of the procession. You can see that the young men are in a hurry to catch up with the others. The position of the horses' heads and necks portray a lively impatience. Notice that Greek riders rode without saddles at this time.

If you look closely, you can see holes in the marble. The bronze bridles and reins that were once there have disappeared. They were probably taken to be melted into weapons for later wars. Even though these sculptures are no longer in perfect condition, it is easy to imagine how elegant they were. They were originally painted in bright colors which have been lost by aging and weathering. Destructive wars and occupying armies added to the damage.

Young Me

These horses were made by unknown Greek artists more than 300 years before the building of the Parthenon. We call this earlier Greek art *Archaic* (ahr-KAY-ic), or ancient. Compare these horses with those from the Parthenon frieze. The four Archaic horses are rigid and without expression. The style of Greek sculpture changed greatly in the 300 years between the making of these frozen figures and the *Young Men on Horseback*, which seem to be in eternal motion.

Archaic Bronze Statuette; about 800 BC; Metropolitan Museum of Art, New York, Rogers Fund.

Relief of a Horseman, Archaic; Courtesy, Museum of Fine Arts, Boston.

Amazon in Combat with a Greek, Archaic; The Louvre, Paris, Photo Alinari.

Black Figure Vase, about 500 BC;
Kunsthistorischen Museum, Vienna.

Amazon on Horseback about 400 BC; by Sotades,
Courtesy, Museum of Fine Arts, Boston.

Vase painters working at about the time of the building of the Parthenon have left us the best examples of Greek drawing and painting. One section of Athens housed the ceramic industry. Vases were made on the potter's wheel and in moulds. The vases had many shapes, and each shape had a specific use. They were made for holding water, oils, foods, perfumes and other items used in the home.

Some painters signed their names to their vases, just as artists do with their paintings today. The subject matter of these vases included scenes from Greek mythology and copies of paintings that have since been destroyed, as well as scenes from the everyday lives of the people. This is one of the best sources we have for learning about ancient Greece.

Vases called *rhytons* (RYE-tahns) were used as drinking cups. This one shows an *Amazon* on horseback. Amazons were fierce female warriors who were supposed to have battled the Greek armies. Other rhytons have been found that are shaped like horses' heads and hoofs.

The Greek city of Pompeii lay buried for hundreds of years under volcanic ash from Mt. Vesuvius (veh-SOO-vee-us). In 1830 archaeologists found this mosaic floor which they believe was made in about 400 BC. It represents a battle scene between Alexander and Darius, and it is thought to be a copy of an earlier Greek painting that has been lost. It is 17 feet long.

The horses shown are full of spirit. The artist was able to show depth in the scene as well as the roundness of each horse. This was done by his choice of slightly different colored pieces of stone.

Detail from the Alexander Mosaic, about 400 BC; Museo Nazionale, Rome, Photo Alinari.

A group of people called the *Etruscans* (i-TRUSS-kins) lived in the midwestern part of Italy as early as the 7th century BC. No one knows the area of their origin. Greek travelers were known to have gone there about the time of the building of the Parthenon. This statue of a rider illustrates some of the Greek ideas in sculpture borrowed by the Etruscans. Greek influence is especially evident in the styling of the hair and in the draping of the clothing. This statue is made of bronze. The horse? No one knows what became of it.

Etruscan Rider, about 500 BC; Detroit Institute of Arts.

When the Romans conquered the Greeks and other peoples of the world they borrowed many ideas. The Roman conquerors saw the horses on the Parthenon. They liked the work of the Greek artists and hired many of them to go to Rome. Although the Roman leaders used the skills of the Greek artists, they did not use all their ideas about style. The Romans wanted as much as possible of the personality and strength of the empire and individuals to be represented by the artists, rather than the Greek idea of general perfection.

The Roman Emperor Marcus Aurelius was the subject for an important equestrian statue. It is a bronze sculpture, larger than life. It is more than 2,000 years old. Michelangelo had it moved in 1538 so that it could be placed in a setting he designed. It is now green with *patina,* a film formed on the surface of the bronze by exposure to weather. It glows warmly where the golden brown of the bronze shows through.

Roman army legions went all through the Empire, which extended over a large part of Europe and Asia and into Africa. A Roman fortress which was uncovered near the German city of Frankfurt on Main is now a museum. This mounted soldier appears on a gravestone, or *steele* (STEEL-ee), which was found at the fortress. This equestrian relief differs from the Roman art as seen in the statue of Marcus Aurelius. It may have been carved by a Roman soldier who always had been on duty in outlying provinces of the far-flung Empire, and who was unaware of the Greek influence in Roman art. We call this artist *provincial* (pruh-VIN-chul), because his work shows little influence by artists in other places.

Roman Soldier on Horseback, about 200 AD; Saalburg Museum, Heddernheim im Taunus, Photo by the author.

Wind Vane from Viking Ship, 9th Century AD; Danish National Museum, Copenhagen.

The Romans called the wandering people of Europe, Asia and Africa *Barbarians* because they were foreigners to the Roman civilization. The Barbarians' art was small in size, because they constantly carried all their possessions from place to place. Art work often decorated their weapons and tools. This bronze horse is one example of Barbarian art from a Viking ship. It was the decoration on the weather vane. The sailors could not have sailed their ships without knowing the direction of the wind. Imagine the bright jewels or stones that shone in this horse's eyes more than 1,000 years ago.

Tomb Tile, Han Dynasty, 206 BC-220 AD; The Art Institute of Chicago, Buckingham collection.

When we look to the East we can see that the ancient artists of Asia worked with the horse perhaps even longer than any of the civilizations we have already discussed. The art of China is many thousands of years old. Very early extant works which were buried with the dead in tombs show us that the Chinese people knew a great deal about working in bronze as well as carving in jade and painting on silk. Chinese artists have always tried to do more than reproduce the actual appearance of a thing. They wanted to portray the inner feeling or "soul" of the subject. Many of the famous Chinese paintings were lost. But the Chinese made reliefs in the style of these paintings, just as the Greeks had made vases.

This relief is from a tomb tile from the Han period which covered about 426 years, from 206 BC to 220 AD. Note that this type of relief was made by using a pointed instrument to draw lines into the wet clay, which was then dried and baked.

Horses were a popular subject in Chinese art during the Tang dynasty which ruled China from 618 to 907 AD. A dynasty is a succession of rulers of one family. An artist named Han Kan was the founder of a school that specialized in portraying horses at that time. These horses from the Tang dynasty were made of pottery and found in tombs. Sometimes the horses' manes and tails were very decorative.

Tomb Horse, Tang Dynasty, 618-907AD; Metropolitan Museum of Art, New York, Gift of Mrs. Edward S. Harkness.

Horse Rubbing Leg, Tang Dynasty; The Art Institute of Chicago, Russell Tyson Collection.

This relief is carved from stone. It comes from the empire of T'ai-tsung (tie-soong), who ruled in the deserts and *steppes* (steps) or prairies of Upper Asia during the Tang dynasty. Historians tell us that this carving illustrates the emperor's yellow-colored battle charger.

Stone Relief, Tang Dynasty; University Museum, Philadelphia.

This rounded figure of a horse was carved in jade. Jade is a semi-precious stone found in many colors. It is a hard stone, difficult to carve. The artist solved the problem by creating a horse that was lying down. With this design he did not have so much hard stone to cut away. The horse was carved about 200 years ago.

Chinese Jade Horse, Ch'ien Lung Dynasty, 1736-1795 AD; Metropolitan Museum of Art, New York, Gift of Samuel T. Peters.

Chinese artists have always been skilled in showing the horse in action. This detail from a painting shows horses being washed in the river. It was painted more than 600 years ago, but you might see the same scene today. The other detail of four horses is believed to have been painted by the same artist.

Four Horses, Attributed to Chao Meng-fu; Metropolitan Museum of Art, New York, The Kennedy Fund.

A painting on a silk scroll tells part of the story of the burning of a Japanese palace. If you look closely and try to count the horses, you will find it nearly impossible. The black horse is typical of the way Japanese artists have shown a galloping horse being controlled by its rider.

The scroll was painted some time between 1200 and 1300 AD. The Japanese artists of this period, called *Kamakura* (ka-ma-COO-rah), tried to show life through realistic detail. This painting gives us the impression that the artist was sitting on a treetop watching a group of riders approaching the palace to set it ablaze.

This type of scroll is called a *makimono* (mah-kee-MO-no). It was never hung up. Sometimes the sheets were folded and bound into an album. Art museums were not known in Japan at that time. Picture scrolls were kept in a chest in the home, to be taken out and studied carefully from time to time.

Burning of Sanjo Palace, Japanese Kamakura School, Mid-13th Century AD; Courtesy, Museum of Fine Arts, Boston.

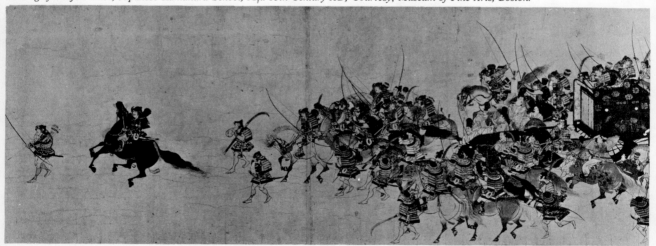

Hokusai (HO-koo-SAH-i) was one of many famous Japanese artists who created horses. In fact, the horse has been so important to the Japanese that one of their calendar years is called "the year of the horse." For more than 2,000 years, believers have offered horses to the religious shrines so that the Japanese gods could ride. These horse offerings have taken many forms. At one time they were clay or terracotta statuettes. Later the actual horse was given to the shrine. Today you can still see the live offspring of these offerings housed in stables that are a part of the shrines. Pictures of horses are now offered to the gods during a festival held on the first day of September of each year at a shrine near Tokyo. Horses have been given so that the gods in the Japanese religion can visit with each other and decide upon the marriages of young girls.

Mother Horse and Foal by Hokusai, 1760-1849; Bibliotheque Nationale, Paris.

This *Mother Horse and Foal,* by Hokusai is a woodcut print. It is one of the few examples we have seen in art up to this time that shows a horse lying down with its young. If you study Hokusai's *technique,* or method of work, you can see that very few lines were used to draw the bodies of the horses.

A sketch for a woodcut is made on a flat wooden board. The artist then carves away the wood that is not part of the design. This leaves a raised picture. The raised surface is inked and then pressed on paper. Each color is printed separately on the same paper by another piece of carved wood.

One of the most popular horses in art history is the one that Saint George rode when he slew the dragon. This particular painting is from Novgorod, Russia. It is called an *icon* (EYE-con), which is a small, portable religious picture. At the time that this painting was done the Russian provinces were isolated from each other because of the Mongol invasions. Novgorod was one city that was not invaded, and icon painting flourished there.

The art that developed in Europe in the Middle Ages was quite different from that of China and Japan. Decoration was needed for the cold and damp stone castles. The art of weaving and embroidering tapestries became popular. Most of these tapestries were hung on the walls to keep out the cold. Some were hung from windows and bridges for celebrations. Scenes on the tapestries often included horses.

The *Bayeux* (by-yuh) *Tapestry* is one such decoration. In 1066 AD, William the Conqueror invaded England. His wife, Queen Matilda, and her ladies-in-waiting embroidered the story of his victory. The complete embroidered tapestry is 231 feet long and 20 inches wide. The needlework was done on brown linen. This work of art contains 1,512 figures, 200 of which are horses. No two figures are alike.   *Detail from Bayeux Tapestry, 11th Century AD; Photo Giraudon.*

Andrea Verrocchio (ver-ROCK-yo) was another artist with two names. His real name was Andrea di Cione, but he preferred being called Verrocchio. He was not only considered a genius in painting, but was also famous as a goldsmith and a sculptor.

Verrocchio's equestrian monument to Bartolommeo Colleoni (co-lee-OH-nee), a military leader, was his last great work before he died in 1488. He was not able to completely finish this sculpture before his death, but his assistants did. They were trained in his workshop and knew his style. It is easy to see the effort Verrocchio put into portraying the movement of a military horse. He created a great sense of straining energy. The horse helps make Bartolommeo Colleoni look important.

Saint George and the Dragon, Novgorod School, Late 14th Century AD; Russian Museum, Leningrad.

Antonio Pisano (pea-SAHN-o), an Italian artist, worked during the period we call the *Renaissance* (REN-uh-SAHNS). The Renaissance started during the 14th century. The name Renaissance means *re-birth*, and was given to this period by those who saw in it a reawakening of man's interest in art, science, and literature after the long sleep of the Dark Ages.

These two mules are an example of Pisano's interest in horses and other animals. Pisano is one of many artists who had two names. You may see some of his work attributed to Pisanello, another form of his name.

Two Mules, by Antonio Pisano (Pisanello), 1395-1450; Archives Photographiques, Paris.

Colleoni, a Military Leader by Andrea Verrocchio, 1435-1488; Venice, Anderson photo.

Leonardo Da Vinci (duh VEEN-chee) is the best-known artist of the Renaissance period. His teacher was Verrocchio. He had many more ideas in art and science than ever could be carried out in his lifetime. Few of his paintings remain, because he often used experimental techniques and materials that did not prove to be durable. Some of his drawings are still available for the world to view, and his horses are included among these.

The drawings you see here may have been made as studies for a colossal bronze statue he was to create in Milan, Italy in 1499. When you look at Da Vinci's horses and compare them to all the other artists' creations up to this time, you can see that Da Vinci knew the horse unusually well. In his studies he actually dissected dead animals so that he could better understand how their bones and muscles were joined. It was said that he had started writing a book on the *anatomy*, or structure, of the horse, but this book was never completed.

Germany also had an "awakening" or Renaissance beginning in the 15th century. One of the famous German artists of the Renaissance is Albrecht Dürer (AHL-brekt DYOOR-er).

This drawing is a line engraving. Dürer ————— sharp, v-shaped tool to carve —— n a copper sheet. Ink was rub- ——— copper plate and then carefully —— surface. The ink remained in —— grooves, and when the plate —— against dampened paper in a —— transferred to the paper. You —— at this process is different from —— in which the artist cuts *away* —— except the lines and areas he —— int. In the line engraving the —— e lines *into* the sheet he wants —— possible to make a great num- —— s with a copper engraving as —— woodcuts.

—— nsidered the greatest original —— ng with this method of print- —— and count the thousands of —— carved or engraved in this cop- —— his picture, printed in black and —— that death is the victor over all —— s.

Many of the artists who have created horses have shown great versatility or ability in creative work other than drawing, painting and sculpture. George Stubbs, an English painter, became interested in horses after he had already established himself in a combined career of lecturing to medical students and painting portraits. It is said that while he was on a journey in 1754 he saw a lion devouring a horse. He became fascinated by the horse, and later wrote a book on the anatomy of this animal.

The major part of the last 46 years of Stubbs' life was devoted to painting animals. The horse was his favorite subject. *Mares and Foals in a Landscape* is one painting typical of the many hundreds George Stubbs completed during his lifetime. The five horses are formed by a series of thousands of fine brush strokes. These have created a graceful round feeling that further lends to the serenity or calm of the scene.

Mares and Foals in a Landscape by George Stubbs, 1724-1800; Tate Gallery, London.

This quickly drawn pen and ink sketch introduces us to a new feeling in art, the art of the 19th century. It is called the *Romantic* movement. Romantic describes a feeling more than a painting technique. Romanticists wanted to record the emotions in life. Sometimes they did it very theatrically with quick strokes that give the viewer the thrill of being involved in the action.

Baron Antoine Jean Gros (grows) was an artist famous for his horsemanship. His pen-and-ink sketch of *Prince Joachim on Horseback* is the record of a proud, rich nobleman who is capable of riding into any situation calling for skill and heroism. The quick, broken pen lines in this drawing gives you the feeling of the rapid, steady movement of the horse.

Prince Joachim on Horseback by Baron Antoine Jean Gros, 1771-1835; Ecole des Beaux Arts, Paris, Photo Giraudon.

Theodore Gericault (zhay-ree-co) is considered the originator of the Romantic movement in France. His work is typified by this horse. It is standing rigidly, frightened by a storm. Gericault is the most famous horse painter of his time. Unfortunately, his death came at the early age of 33. The cause? Injuries suffered in a fall from the animal he loved the most—a horse.

A Horse Frightened by Lightning by Theodore Gericault, 1791-1824; National Gallery, London.

Horse, 1828, by Eugene Delacroix, 1798-1863; Archives Photographiques, Paris.

Eugene Delacroix (del-ah-cwah) was another important Romantic painter in France. His print of a quickly-moving horse makes you share the feeling of the horse's hurry. He shows fear of some force we cannot see.

The oil painting of the two horses coming out of the sea illustrates the lively impatience of horses who have just bathed and frolicked in the water. Their movements do not show the fear we saw in the first picture. *Horses Coming out of the Sea, 1860, by Eugene Delacroix; Phillips Collection, Washington, D. C.*

Most of Honore Daumier's (on-aw-ray dome-yay) work was devoted to making social and political protests and commentaries. This classifies his as a Romanticist, recording emotion in life. In fact, one cartoon landed him in prison when he offended King Louis Philippe by illustrating him as Gargantua devouring the people.

The drawing we see here, *Immigrants*, is typical of his feelings of sympathy and compassion shown through his art. *The Horsemen* further illustrates his ability to tell much with but a few brush strokes.

Immigrants by Honore Daumier, 1808-1879; Ecole des Beaux Arts, Paris, Photo Giraudon.

The Horsemen by Honore Daumier; Courtesy, Museum of Fine Arts, Boston.

The Horse Fair, 1853-1855, by Rosa Bonheur, 1822-1899; Metropolitan Museum of Art, New York, Gift of Cornelius Vanderbilt.

The Horse Fair is one of the most famous horse paintings made by a woman. This work is a large oil painting. The canvas is approximately 8 feet by 17 feet in size. Rosa Bonheur (bun-urr), its creator, lived in France. Her work reflects the Romantic movement. When you look at the painting and see the many large black horses and grey horses being raced around in a circle, do you want to rub your eyes to remove the dust the horses kick up as they sweep by?

English Promenade at Nice, 1879-1881, by Henri de Toulouse-Lautrec, 1864-1901;

Henri de Toulouse-Lautrec (too-looz loh-trek) was a French painter who had a style all his own. His versatility in drawing and his special interest in horses are shown in this picture of a quickly-moving horse and carriage. It was first drawn with a pencil and then painted with watercolor. Notice how few strokes he needed to give the feeling of motion.

Horses played an important role in the lives of the settlers and Indians of the United States. *The Buffalo Hunter* was painted in about 1830 by an unknown American artist. The painting is about three and one-half feet by four feet in size. We have seen hunters and horses in art before, but few artists have shown the quick courage demonstrated by this brave Indian hunter and his horse.

Buffalo Hunter, about 1830, Anonymous American; Santa Barbara Museum of Art.

Another unknown American carved this wooden horse that stands approximately two feet high. It is more than 100 years old and has lost its horsehair tail, but can't you imagine how frisky the horse looked in front of a harness-maker's shop? Its head has an expressiveness similar to the horses we saw on the Parthenon.

Wooden Shop Sign, Early 19th Century, Anonymous American; University of Nebraska Museum, Lincoln, Collection of the Nebraska Art Association.

American Romantic artists recorded the importance of horses in 19th century American life. This scene was painted in Bowling Green, New York by David Johnson. It shows the center of town on a sunny day in Spring.

Bowling Green, 1860, by David Johnson; New York Historical Society, New York City.

Max Klepper, another 19th century American Romanticist, painted the *Route of the Four-Horse Coach "Liberty."* The bridge the coach is crossing was on the route near Turkey Blue Ball, New Jersey.

Recording history has often been the role of artists, especially before the widespread use of photographs. With this painting, Klepper helped record the important role horses played in the American transportation system of the 19th century.

Four-Horse Coach "Liberty," 19th Century, by Max Klepper; New York Historical Society, New York City.

Thomas Sully was born at the close of the American Revolution. George Washington was one of the popular heroes of the time and an excellent subject for a Romantic painter. Sully imagined this scene which he painted long after Washington's death. George Washington looks younger here than he ever appeared in portraits for which he actually posed. Sully's main interest was in painting portraits of famous people in England and the United States. He may not have known so much about painting horses as he did about flattering people. This may be why the horse seems rather stiff.

George Washington by Thomas Sully, 1783-1872; The Union League of Philadelphia.

Frederick Remington portrayed the glamour and everyday life of the American West. This bronze statue of *The Bronco Buster* was created in 1909, at the beginning of the 20th century—*our* century. The statue stands nearly three feet high and gives us an exciting account of a battle between man and horse. This record in bronze preserves a rapidly disappearing part of American life for future viewers.

The Bronco Buster, 1909, by Frederick Remington, 1861-1909; Philbrook Art Center, Tulsa.

Edgar Degas (duh-gah), a French artist, was also interested in preserving the activities of the horse in sculpture. This bronze statue is about one foot in size, but it gives us an excellent idea of the horse in action. You can actually see the start of the horse's jump. Degas' horse doesn't have any ears or mane. The artist wanted to give you the feeling of the jump, and details were not important.

Horse Clearing an Obstacle, 1881, by Edgar Degas, 1834-1917; Tate Gallery, London.

Franz Marc, a German, was one of a group of artists called *Expressionists* who rebelled against what was going on in the art world around them. The hustle and bustle and worries of the city disturbed Marc. He wanted to concentrate on the calmer and less disturbing aspects of life. Animals were his favorite subjects.

These horses were painted in many shades of blue, because Marc felt that this color helped show the harmony and rhythm of nature. If you look at the whole length of the canvas with a quick glance, you can see the sweeping rhythm of the wide blue curved brush strokes. *Blue Horses,*

1911, by Franz Marc, 1880-1916; Walker Art Center, Minneapolis.

Raoul Dufy (rah-ool dyoo-fee) loved bright colors. His full-time profession was designing textiles for a French fashion designer, but he preferred painting. *Chateau and Horses,* an oil painting, seems to combine his talents. It could be part of a pattern on drapery material we see today. Dufy was especially famous for these gay landscapes. If you examine his work closely you can see that Dufy painted with sure, quick brush strokes. Just a few strokes created the impression of a very strong and fast carriage horse.

Chateau and Horses, 1930, by Raoul Dufy, 1877-1953; Phillips Collection, Washington, D. C.

Henry Moore, the famous English sculptor, sometimes feels out his ideas in quick sketches. These three very rapidly drawn pen-and-ink sketches show us one of the many ways in which great art can be created by the artist as he translates what he sees and imagines. Henry Moore knows the horse. In fact, he knows it so well that he needs but a few simple lines to show it to us. Moore is also known as a fine *draftsman,* or a person who draws well.

Henry Moore, 1898- ; Sketches, ©George Rainbird Ltd., London.

Another artist, also famous for sculpture, uses the horse in practically all of his work. Marino Marini works in bronze. He is one of few *contemporary*, or present day, well-known artists who portray people with animals. This horse and rider statuette is less than one foot high.

Horseman, 1901, by Marino Marini; University of Nebraska Museum, Lincoln, F. M. Hall Collection.

Not all of Marini's work is small. This horse and rider stands to a height of six feet, nearly life-size. Does it remind you of the Archaic Greek horses and riders from about 800 BC?

Artists may all be different, but they do have much in common. Art from the past influences working artists today. In another two thousand years, will visitors to art museums compare their work to Marini's?

Horse and Rider, 1949, by Marino Marini; Walker Art Center, Minneapolis.

LIST OF PHOTOGRAPHS

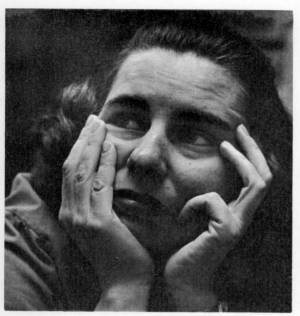

Bonnee Fleming

ABOUT THE AUTHOR

Ruth Zuelke holds a Master of Arts degree in art education from the University of Minnesota. She has taught at the St. Paul Gallery Art School, the Minneapolis Vocational Evening School, and the University of Minnesota Laboratory High School. Her study and research programs have included extensive travels abroad. She has spent five years in Europe, one and a half years in the Orient, and has visited Mexico numerous times. This varied background in the art of different cultures, together with her painstaking research, has well qualified Miss Zuelke to author a study on the horse in art history.

ABOUT THE DESIGNER

Robert Clark Nelson is a distinguished designer with extensive achievements to his credit. He is a graduate of the Minneapolis School of Arts and Bethel College, and is currently an instructor in art, painting and graphic design at the latter institution.

Mr. Nelson's work has been included in five editions of the *Graphic Annual*, and two editions of the *New York Art Directors Annual*. His most recent honor has been the inclusion of four of his posters in the *International Poster Annual*, a Swiss publication covering the poster art of 26 countries.